The Lonely Street Laundromat

Wade Villani

First published in Australia by Aurora House

This edition published in Australia by Aurora House 2023
www.aurorahouse.com.au
Copyright © 2023

Typesetting and e-book design: Cognition Technology |
www.cognition-technology.com
Cover Designer: Donika Mishineva | www.artofdonika.com

ISBN number: 978-1-922913-21-0 (paperback)

A catalogue record for this
book is available from the
National Library of Australia

NATIONAL
LIBRARY
OF AUSTRALIA

Distributed by: *Ingram Content*: www.ingramcontent.com
Australia: *Phone*: +613 9765 4800 |
Email: lsiaustralia@ingramcontent.com
Milton Keynes UK: *Phone*: +44 (0)845 121 4567 |
Email: enquiries@ingramcontent.com
La Vergne, TN USA: *Phone*: +1 800 509 4156 |
Email: inquiry@lightningsource.com

Mum

For the pleasure of each word to each poem
a pleasure only allowed me from the perspectives
you've given me.
A warmer palm to grasp for guidance
there has been none. All my love and appreciation
this book is yours and each after.

The Lonely Street
Laundromat

I'm bed linen come to life.

I'm goose feather and quilt – too many pillows. Unlovable piece of shit.

I can't be loved; how many broken hearts must weep upon me? Fractured pane, glance through.

Fractured fucking pane, don't look within lest your eyes be cut and bled. Tumble dry – shrink to size.

I don't fit in my own skin.

Tossing and turning; a waking nightmare.

All linens, cotton and clenching fists with bleeding palms. The Lonely Street Laundromat.

My prison.

Negative image silhouetted fears pressed to grey clouded sky.

Angels' wings echo

amid the soundless approaching night and the dark blurs as if submerged.

Finding refuge among the vines. With burning feet and skip-less step.

To escape the responsibility,

to escape the disinterested stares that young boy with the curly hair he creates worlds to escape, but cannot reach them.

Those lilac sands and nebulous skies not his world

but a not so distant one,

the blade between index and thumb like a small doorway to crawl through and the key,

press deep into the wrist.

What price too high to pay him, the Ferryman

that patient Gatekeeper.

Pleasure like a disturbed awakening.
To feel the untold screams within,
countless and merging to that unified voice:
"You aren't loved".
Then begins the hunt of hedonism.
Fill the cracks in the pavement with crushed leaves,
pray the rains don't come.

I allow my shadow to devour the light.

I stand pensive,

allowing loneliness to swallow me. The encroaching breeze that dissolves,

as I'm grasping at the sleeves of passers-by.

Heart humming through my mouth, just take me with you.

Push me into pockets of loose change and filters, I won't be a nuisance,

just allow the loneliness to digest me. I'll sink into gravel path,

become the gloom behind the streetlamp. Less human, more ether.

Let me be the ether you breathe

exhale me.

Solemnity.

Iridescent light shatters shadows beneath
and the evergreen blends with the clouds.
The sky moments from opening it seems,
I stand not asleep, but in a dream.
Sometimes to glimpse behind the curtain,
You need only look at the breeze.

I'm having that beginnings feeling.

The enormous responsibility that comes with the words. The ones uttered between the sheets,

those uttered with that impending need, that glee.

Can you not see

where nature itself blends. Taking that form,

freckled shoulders and dimpled back.

Inevitably through the streets, over the speed bumps and ending here at the door

begging you to open up.

As you lay in bed with another less freckly pair of shoulders.

A cry for those days spent well with you.

Trees walk like men through the pavilion,
grass grows up clinging to pant legs.

The light inside just a little dimmer,
while the dark is blinding bright.
The deafening night.

Kangaroos bounce the bitumen at dusk.

I ride parallel, which is which.
Truly untethered.

Bright red sky – atmosphere alight.
I strain to enter the bright
to see between the trees
on this in-between-destination street.

Fucking enigma.

Appearing in my memories, peripheral hallucinations.

Hairs on the back of my neck, I feel you there.

Can't I escape you, creeping from sleep to waking world? Creaking boards down the hall as you make your way.

I dust you from the tabletop, bleach you from the sheets

yet you linger here without cause. Where is my refuge from you?

This purgatory of my own design. I am the enigma.

The hallucination.

In the dark I raise my blinds just a little to let the light in.

Feeling the cold streetlamp on my skin is to anchor reality.

The observation of the continuation of life without me.

I am not a piece of the puzzle, I am the space between.

The dark line, the absence of image.

A cosmic blackhole the size of a human heart.

There is a lonely street

parallel to the train tracks that head out of town.

Here there's a flag that dances with the wind in its grasp

        the energy of the inanimate.

This piece of adorned material pirouettes, almost free of its earthly bounds.

Each fibre reaching for the neighbouring tree,

together they sway and speak of a world atop our own. This world of the ethereal that whispers life to all.

There is a lonely street

parallel to the train tracks that head out of town.

Here a woman sits unmoving behind her desk

        the lethargy of the animate.

This human unique, undesigned seeks not beyond her earthly bounds.

Ignorant of the ether just beyond her window.

You're a small fly
furiously fighting its end atop the window
ledge.
A mouse
unknowing of the poison in its belly.
A twinkle
in the night sky already extinguished. You
just don't know it.
Yet.

The overweight oligarchy with festering
wounds.

The lads at the bar on the prowl.

Illusions of bliss, rainbows within
teardrops.

Fist full of sand, pour through fingers.

Scream at the wind.

The bartender slides the drink across the
bar top,

one extra ingredient.

Lightning hits dry crop.

Heat meets air; meets testosterone at the
bar

and solipsism sips that soured cider.

A beauty sleeps, fairy tales cross.

What big fangs you have.

Illusions of misery, hot breath on the back
of an

unwilling neck.

Heel broken, bruised thigh.

Snow White blamed for going out tonight.

This primordial soup isn't quite ready,
needs a little more solicitude.

The Earth claims no victory over we.

She smites us down
decomposes our flesh, and
our bones too are turned to dust.
As she
spins and wobbles,
eons of dance,
that cosmic tango.
Empires to rise and fall
while she quietly awaits.

Put your hand to the dirt,
listen carefully
you can hear her careless ease.

Feel the Earth between your toes,
the rebirth of your soul.

These lovely, quiet, insignificant things.
Always toiling zealously toward.

The wind passes over and through them,
as if without regard.

But these lovely things wish to be known,
so they create more of themselves
and beat their chests to protest the
nothings.
Their creations are like them,
searching for meaning where there is none.
Search elsewhere tiny things.

For the cocoon cannot be broken from the
outside,
lest the creature within is too weak to
survive the world.

What is real?
If the light we see can be distorted and
refracted
by drops of rain on a pine branch.
And a billion years after a star has died
it still calls to us in the night.

Breathe in the sun.

Breathe out the moon.

Walk your way through the clouds,

Reality tugs at your ankles, but you continue the climb.

Fingers tight around quasars, you raise yourself up.

Step out of conscious space, you're in that new place.

The lights here contrived, aligned.

That flavour of future awakenings.

The allegory of the cave,

Now explain this other place.

Those displaced shadows beyond the mouth of the gallery.

What is reality?

Am I just the butterfly dreaming I'm a man?

Our happiness is a transitory thing.
Dandelion seeds adrift and searching,
Nature's flavour bittersweet, near sour.
Scrunch up your mouth at the thought of it.
Sometimes happiness is unimaginable,
other times we are engulfed by it,
consumed so fully misery becomes myth.
Seeds in fertile soil then germinate,
grow miraculous things, from near
nothings.
Strong and stable, stalk pulled from the
Earth
and the tiny world of angelic spores are
dispersed
by a single breath.
Sometimes that's all it takes.
A single breath,
to leave us adrift and searching once more.

Today the cloudless sky permits the moon to dwell amongst the day.

That cratered crescent, a homage to all beautiful things.

However out of place they may seem.

Now.
So, when is now?
In all time passed and to come, it is.
You will and you were, later and before.
So, when is now?
Now.

Young soul.

Bull – china shop
Learn the world without regard.
Grow – evolve
With chaos in your wake.
Your clay is yet to meet the kiln,
yet I see your shape.

Young soul.
What lessons did I teach you?

You don't intimidate me baby.
I'm the rising tide that takes the shore,
the raging wind turning land to dust.
I'm the raw.
The untamed, unnamed.

Orange hued horizon screams for the day
to end.

Softly dissolving clouds echo glorious pink
and gold

to the furthest reaches of the evening sky.

The birds complete their daily pilgrimage

to arrive home upon their everchanging
perch.

Sol and Luna fight for dominion,

culminating in that deluge of dark.

Cyclical predictability.

Is it always this predictable?

There's a laundromat on the corner of a
perpetually For Sale lot,

a place that sings into the night on this
in-between-destination street.

Here there is a consciousness.

Hands in warm linen she smiles past me at
the waxing moon,

frizzy hair bunned and makeup undone,

she exists only here.

And I'm that lonely, forgotten sock under a
charming, rusted chair

Not a care.

Let's be scolded or freezing

let's dip our toes in the swell, hand to sun-
kissed skin.

Let's greet each other naked at the door and
make love in the middle of the street.

You can look directly at the sun to feel that
ether

or maybe hold my hand, kiss to the
corner of my mouth.

You love like you think it'll kill you, but
you don't mind.

Toes meet under the protection of morning
light and

frosty breath meets in that warm exchange.

We can never be just right

let's be scolded or freezing.

Fuck seeking out the meaning.

When I can seek the curves of you beside
me.

Where edges seem to merge, I ask

where am I? and where are you?

Let's be scolded or freezing.

She looked at me

and from those perpetually pursed lips
whispered,

those haunting words of her sojourn
soliloquy.

The clouds opened above her head,

from them fell the autumn leaves.

Cupped hands full, she feeds me that
bloom.

In awe I reach deep into my pockets,

I pull out my own wilted leaves.

Eyes torn from sockets; I see her clearly
now.

That enclave in flesh, that nation of her
own.

Still looking at me her eyes too are gone.

Yet I've never felt more seen.

You lay there
stardust shimmering in the starlight.
The sun seeming to kiss you on the cheek,
a blessed thing with all the permissions of
the cosmos.

You wake to the eight squares of light upon
your bedroom wall.
That light ether upon you like a physical
embrace.
You wish to be as weightless and carefree as
those
dust particles dancing in the sunlight.

To me,
you exist only here.
My memory upon revisiting thoughts of
you
allows me only the fictional, the layered
reality.
An idea.
Is that all you are,
laid out on those terracotta linen sheets,
sun hitting your cheeks.
What an idea.

A truly symphonic existence.

Leaves from branch to sleet,

wind guiding descent like an omniscient hand.

There is a rhythm here in the unbridled

the untouched free expression.

Does this reside only here – only now – only so that I may observe it?

Not through sleep or screen, consciousness present completely.

That beginnings feeling, upon me again.

You sit within your box
scintillating only for yourself.
Yet the trees, they see you
they admire your sturdy footing
and the oceans, they see you
remarking upon your glorious ebb and flow.
The cosmos cannot replicate you,
Unique and everlasting are the atoms
that miraculously came together.
Like a whisper into cupped hands,
you are here.
You exist infinitely within your time.

Flames shackled by wax and wick
as the night creeps in through the cracked
pane.
The Spider weaves its tapestries here.

In this moment,
it's as if the night will never wane.
Allowing the flame to exist perpetually.
To not disappear like stars in the day,
to allow the spider to weave its universe
into fruition.
Weave the whole world on your endless
night my arachnid friend

and I shall weave mine.

About the Author

I see what others can't or choose not to.

I grew up feeling as though no one would ever know me and now, nearing 30, I realise I was right. I am a candle that flickers in the forest without observation, who's to say I'm there.

This anthology chronicles an ascent that was ultimately lifesaving. Without the observations, influence and ether that I've described across these few pages I would surely be dead. The privilege of life, while puzzlingly painful, is one that I'm not quite ready to rid myself of. To those who seek solace here I ask that you turn your gaze within, the glory and awe you seek is upon your lips with each breath.

Thank you for reading.